XL MACHINES!

BULLDOZERS

SETH KINGSTON

PowerKiDS press™

New York

Published in 2020 by The Rosen Publishing Group, Inc.
29 East 21st Street, New York, NY 10010

First Edition

Editor: Elizabeth Krajnik
Book Design: Michael Flynn

Photo Credits: Cover, p. 1 SERGEI PRIMAKOV/Shutterstock.com; series background (dirt) exopixel/Shutterstock.com; p. 5 Smileus/Shutterstock.com; pp. 7, 17 Yevhen Anistrat/Shutterstock.com; p. 9 Alexander Levitsky/Shutterstock.com; p. 11 Miljan Zivkovic/Shutterstock.com; p. 13 (straight blade) Zhao jian kang/Shutterstock.com; p. 13 (universal blade) bondgrunge/Shutterstock.com; p. 15 JVrublevskaya/Shutterstock.com; p. 19 (main) AButyrin 22/Shutterstock.com; p. 19 (inset) asadykov/Shutterstock.com; p. 21 Grant Terry/Shutterstock.com; p. 22 Nerthuz/Shutterstock.com.

Cataloging-in-Publication Data
Names: Kingston, Seth.
Title: Bulldozers / Seth Kingston.
Description: New York : PowerKids Press, 2020. | Series: XL machines! | Includes glossary and index.
Identifiers: ISBN 9781725311381 (pbk.) | ISBN 9781725311404 (library bound) | ISBN 9781725311398 (6pack)
Subjects: LCSH: Bulldozers–Juvenile literature. | Earthmoving machinery–Juvenile literature.
Classification: LCC TA725.K56 2020 | DDC 629.225–dc23
Manufactured in the United States of America

CPSIA Compliance Information: Batch #CSPK19. For Further Information contact Rosen Publishing, New York, New York at 1-800-237-9932.

CONTENTS

Big Machines!

Bulldozers are big machines! They're often bright colors, and they make loud noises. You can find them in many places, such as roadwork sites, **construction** sites, and farms. Bulldozers have important jobs. Seeing them in action is **exciting**!

What Do Bulldozers Do?

Bulldozers are used to push earth and rocks. They can also dig into the ground and spread **material** around. Some people use bulldozers to remove trees and large rocks, too. Bulldozers are often used with other heavy machinery.

Parts of a Bulldozer

A bulldozer is made up of a heavy steel blade or plate at the front of a tractor. The tractor may have four wheels or it may be a crawler. Crawlers have metal tracks. Crawler bulldozers are more common.

Why Tracks?

The wide metal tracks on crawler bulldozers help them move over different types of ground easily. They also help spread the weight of the bulldozer evenly across the ground so it doesn't sink in. Bulldozers can be very heavy!

Types of Blades

Bulldozers can have different kinds of blades. Straight blades are short and don't curve. These blades are used for making the ground even. Universal blades are tall with a very curved top and side wings. These can push large amounts of material.

universal blade

straight blade

13

S-U Blades

Combination blades have smaller side wings and less of a top curve. They're a combination, or mix, of a straight blade and a universal blade. Some people call them S-U blades. S-U blades are often used to push large rocks in **quarries**.

Blade Movements

Bulldozer blades can move in a number of ways. Some can move side to side, lift, and tip. Four-way blades move left, right, up, and down. However, they can't tip. Six-way blades move in almost any way you can think of. They can tip.

The Ripper

Some bulldozers have a ripper on the back. This **device** turns and breaks up tightly packed earth or other material. Some rippers are made of just one tooth-like piece called a shank. Other rippers have two or more shanks.

Biggest Bulldozer

In the 1980s, Umberto Acco built the ACCO super dozer. It's more than 40 feet (12.2 m) long and weighs 183 tons (166 mt). Its blade is 23 feet (7 m) wide and 9 feet (2.7 m) high. The ripper is 10 feet (3.1 m) tall.

Dozers at Work

Bulldozers do important work. Without them, it would be much harder to move large amounts of earth, build roads, take down old buildings, and make the ground even. Can you picture a world without these extra-large machines?

GLOSSARY

construction: The act or process of building something, such as a house or road.

device: A tool used for a certain purpose.

exciting: Causing feelings of interest and enthusiasm.

material: Something from which something else can be made.

quarry: A place where people dig for stone for building.

INDEX

WEBSITES

Due to the changing nature of Internet links, PowerKids Press has developed an online list of websites related to the subject of this book. This site is updated regularly. Please use this link to access the list: www.powerkidslinks.com/xlm/bulldozers